Redirecting
THE OUT-OF-CONTROL CHILD

Eliminate Defiance & Talking Back Without Using
Punishments, Time-Outs, Behavioral Plans, or Rewards!

JASON K. JOHNSON
www.theinhomeparentcoach.com

DISCLAIMER
Redirecting the Out-of Control Child offers practical advice from Jason Johnson's Behavioral Emotional and Supportive Thoughts Parent Leadership Model™ (B.E.S.T. Parent Leadership Model™). This model focuses on the behavior patterns of children and how to effectively parent using verbal/nonverbal communication and leadership skills. Please be advised that the techniques in this program are not considered therapy, nor is the advice in this book meant to replace receiving therapy, counseling, or medical treatment from a trained and licensed mental health or healthcare professional.

The tips and advice offered in this book, including, without limitation, any advice on handling your children, is undertaken at your sole discretion. Should you decide to follow all or any part of the advice provided in this manual, or should you require your children to follow any instructions provided in this program, you and they do so entirely at your own risk, and by voluntarily undertaking such risk, you hereby release Jason Johnson from any and all claims, actions, damages, obligations, or liabilities based upon any acts or (omissions of acts) in connection with the advice provided herein.

The In-Home Parent Coach® makes no promises or guarantees regarding the outcome of the situation for which you have sought advice. Children exhibiting signs of danger to self or others should be placed under the care of a qualified professional.

Copyright © 2011 Jason K. Johnson
All rights reserved. No part of this program (including written materials, audio materials, live in-home parent leadership training materials, etc.) may be reproduced, stored in a retrieval system, transmitted, in any form or by any means, without written permission from the author of this book.

ISBN: 0615481310
ISBN-13: 9780615481319

*In loving memory of my brother, father, mother, and grandmother.
I love you all and miss you very much...*

And to my most important teachers: the children and parents I have served over the years. You have brought out the best in me to share these valuable lessons, and helped me become the man I am today.

Dear Parents,

Do you love your child? Of course you do! That is why (as far as I am concerned) you will never need a single parenting skill! For knowing how to love your child/children, you are already the expert, and nobody can ever teach you how to do that!

Unfortunately, love alone does not guarantee that your child will:

- Follow directions without talking back;
- Stop using physical aggression towards others;
- Be ready for school/bed on time;
- Share their toys with their siblings;
- Refrain from tantrums;
- Become accountable for their actions.

But something in addition to love does! What does it take to get my child to cooperate better?

Leadership Training.

That's right, leadership training. You see, it is neither your fault nor your child's that parenting is so challenging.

The reality is that a breakdown has occurred in parent-child relationships due to the fast pace, technologically advanced, high-pressure world we live in today.

To make matters worse, very little training, guidance, or assistance is available (other than advice from family and friends, self-help books, therapy, residential, and hospital treatment for extreme cases).

We have so many technological advancements; and yet, we are left with only a few answers to critical questions.

Questions, such as:

- How do I get my child to listen the first time?
- How do I get my children to stop bickering and whining?
- How do I motivate my child without nagging, yelling, or punishing?

I am Jason Johnson, the In-Home Parent Coach. I have spent many years working with hundreds of challenging toddlers through teenagers diagnosed with A.D.H.D, Oppositional Defiance Disorder, Conduct Disorder, Asperger's Syndrome, and Bipolar. I work with boys and girls (ages 2-19) with *severe* emotional/behavioral issue from various ethnic backgrounds, races, and religions.

I created *Redirecting the Out-of-Control Child: Eliminate Defiance & Talking Back without Using Punishments, Time-Outs, Behavioral Plans, or Rewards* from the overwhelming need for parents to have the necessary skills to handle their children's most challenging behaviors.

From managing tantrums, to limiting acting out, or even violent behaviors, parents will learn step-by-step how to drastically shorten the weeks (sometimes months or even years) it takes to restore order in the home, strengthen the bond between parent/child, and reconnect with your child-tonight!

Sincerely,

Jason Johnson

Jason K. Johnson
(The In-Home Parent Coach)
www.theinhomeparentcoach.com

Table of Contents

INTRODUCTION xi

CHAPTER 1 1
Punishments Don't Work

CHAPTER 2 3
Time-Outs Are a Waste of Time

CHAPTER 3 5
Behavioral Plans Decrease Problem-Solving Skills

CHAPTER 4 9
Rewards Stunt Growth of Intrinsic Motivation

CHAPTER 5 13
Parent as Leader

CHAPTER 6 17
Communication

CHAPTER 7 29
Needs vs. Wants

CHAPTER 8 35
How Children Learn

CHAPTER 9 43
The Mind Shift

CHAPTER 10 49
The New Presentation

CHAPTER 11 69
Deliberate Practice

CHAPTER 12 75
Proper Feedback

CHAPTER 13 77
Steps to End Defiance and Talking Back— Tonight

CHAPTER 14 97
Effectively Leading Conversations

CHAPTER 15 103
Conclusion The Marathon

Introduction

After working with hundreds of extremely difficult children, teens, and young adults (ages 2-19), I have finally come up with a wonderful strategy to "fix" their "bad" behavior—forever!

Want to know how? Of course you do, and I would love to share it with you. It works 100 percent of the time, and it never fails. The secret is simple, and here it is... (Drum roll please)...

Changing myself changes the child

It is a revolutionary way to look at how to handle a child's difficult behavior because there is just no way around it...ever!

If you are reading this manual with the hope that you do not have to change yourself and that a magic spell is available that puts your child into a "trancelike" state to do whatever you say, whenever, then the best of luck on your quest. That spell does not exist!

But if you are willing to learn the life-changing skills that will leave your child with no other choice but to follow your lead, this may be the last manual you will ever need!

No more parenting books? That's right! You will have no need for other strategies because in this book you will learn how to be as *powerful* a parent as one of the *strongest* elements on this Earth...

WATER

Did you say water? Yes...Water. Water is so *powerful* that it can erode mountains and even kill thousands of people in a tsunami... And yet...it is *flexible* enough to take on the shape of any container. Think about that for a moment.

Reading this manual will help you to be like "water." Ultimately you will gain the power, the flexibility, and the leadership skills necessary to change yourself, and shortly after, your child.

Let us begin the journey of **self-transformation** now...

Chapter 1
Punishments Don't Work

So let's take a look at punishments. Punishments are something that has haunted humankind since the beginning of time. It dates back to biblical times, with an "eye for an eye" and a "tooth for a tooth."

Punishments have wreaked havoc over the history of humankind, and all the creative ways we figured how to punish people. Instead of talking about how we've developed the punishment system, I would like to first talk about what a punishment is.

I define punishment as the **deliberate retaliation** for an offense by inflicting **physical and/or emotional pain**. That's very interesting. Why in the world would anybody want to deliberately inflict physical and/or emotional pain on his or her child?

Well, the truth is real simple. We don't really want to hurt them; it just turns out that is all we know how to do. It's very typical for parents when they get frustrated and things aren't going their way: they'll start raising their voices, they'll start yelling, and some parents will even spank/hit.

Why in the world does this happen? Somewhere along the way "somebody" decided that the best way to teach someone something is to smack him/her, inflict some kind of pain, or to take away something that will hurt his/her feelings.

Now some people will argue that over the years that we've used punishments they have worked. I don't agree. When children are punished, either physically or emotionally, a very interesting thing happens.

Instead of the "lesson" that was "supposed" to be learned, children are physically hurt, (others have their favorite toys taken from them), and what actually happens is they no longer focus on what they did wrong. Instead, children start placing the blame **outside** them, and they will **make excuses** for acting out.

Three **major problems** arise, on top of the fact that children do not have the problem-solving skills to begin with. If emotional or physical pain is inflicted, that leaves children without

> Getting their needs met,
> Knowing how to solve the problem,
> Knowing what to do differently in the future

That is why punishments are really a very dangerous thing. Punishments give a "rite of passage" for children to not be **accountable** for their **actions**. Why? Because the child was **hurt**, whether it was physical or emotional doesn't matter to children.

Chapter 2
Time-Outs Are a Waste of Time

The second strategy that most parents and teachers are very familiar with is the use of time-outs. I particularly get a kick out of the concept of a time-out.

Basically, time-outs are used when a child is doing something that they're not supposed to, so they sit in a chair and something **miraculously** happens. The child will come out of the chair, say "I'm sorry," and then **never** do it again.

Truth be told, this is what adults believe works. For example, if a child who punches somebody in the face or takes another child's toy is placed in a chair for "one minute per age," then after "doing time" the child will know what to do differently next time. This is really **absurd** to me.

Especially when you add what "experts" **don't** tell parents in the literature. When you read about time-outs, they don't tell you about the **power struggle** to get your child **into time-out**. That's just problem number one.

Number two, these experts don't tell you how to get them to **stay in time out**. It becomes a power struggle to bring your child back and forth, lugging the child over to the chair, corner, etc. Then, you start to ask questions, like "**how** do I keep my child **in** time-out?"

So what do the gurus say? The literature says "tell them if they don't stay in their chair, then you will add minutes to their time out." Or even better, the time-out will not begin until the child is sitting still.

As we've all seen on *Super Nanny*—and as we've seen **in general** through our own experience—time-outs **last forever**. Something that should be **two to ten minutes** turns into **hours**. What's the point of that?

Do you really think that **hours later** your child will have a clue as to why he/she punched another child in the first place? Do you know why you're sitting there **wrestling** back and forth with your child? No, it becomes a **complete mess**!

A mess…and let me tell you, I've been there. I didn't just come up with this overnight and say "I think time-outs are worthless." I actually had to go through a whole stage where I used time-outs all the time. I would do **hundreds** of time-outs a week for children in a therapeutic/behavioral school.

When I took a step back, I finally started to see that I was causing one power struggle after another power struggle, and it just **didn't** make sense!

Chapter 3

Behavioral Plans Decrease Problem-Solving Skills

Behavioral plans and rewards systems also don't make sense. I'm going to discuss them together for part of this chapter because they're really easier to handle as a pair. Some experts are going to be upset because tons of behavioral plans and reward systems are floating around out there.

From token economies, to charts, to point systems...you name it and they have it. You can earn "one hundred points" and you can save up for "rinky-dink" toy, favorite treat, or something else that your child will use for seventy-two hours and **never again**. You do sense the sarcasm, which derives from my knowledge of the history of behaviorism, and I'd like to shed a little light on it.

Go back about seventy to ninety years when the forefathers of behaviorism did something very interesting: they ran lots and lots of tests on animals. They figured if they could control an animal's behavior, then they could link it to how to control human behavior. It was interesting, in theory, but most of it was done on rats, pigeons, dogs, and cats.

As time went by, it started to be used for children in school systems. How in the world did that happen? Well, let me tell you why they were using animals in the **first place**.

First, there's this something called **inhumane**. You see, you can't take a human life and purposefully mess with it. You can't do things like they used to do to cats, like **starve them** and use **sleep deprivation**, and do all sorts of other stuff!

Experimenters were not allowed to test humans that way. Plus, no adults (or children) existed **naturally in the world** with certain problems to enable testing them.

That's **why** experiments had to rely on cats, dogs, and other animals. No children were **naturally** sleep deprived to help the experimenters figure out how human nature works.

Instead, what experimenters did was hundreds and thousands of tests on animals and concluded, "If it works for animals, then it **has to** work for children."

Basically, today we're using the methods of **dog training** to raise children. We tell our children "come" and "sit," and we use the punishments and rewards that it takes to **train an animal**. Now, I understand human beings **are** animals, but we have much more going for us than dogs, cats, and all those cool animals in movies. Yet we're still using those *same strategies* to get our children to behave.

Now I didn't explain how behavioral plans made it into school systems, and why today everywhere you look it's behaviorism, charts, and behavioral plans. Well, I'll tell you. One of the founding fathers of behaviorism realized that creating a "hope of gain" and a "fear of loss" in humans could be used in advertising to **make money**.

So this behaviorist, who was an academic and a scholar, brought this idea to an advertising agency, and he was so happy and excited he had this new way of "reaching people" and controlling their behavior. Interestingly enough, the world of advertisement **laughed at him**. Why in the world did they laugh at him?

They laughed at him because in advertising they had known this for **hundreds of years**. Advertisers had been using hope of gain and fear of loss to shape people's **buying** behaviors! This was **not** a new concept.

Unfortunately for that poor behaviorist, who became very famous, he had to leave advertising, and he was shunned. But not in academics; you see, he was a **big time** professor! He was able to use his pull in academics to teach the academic world how you can control human behavior.

There was only one problem: it was built on a foundation of cards; it was built on a foundation that you can shape animal behavior and apply that to human behavior. The truth is you **just can't**. Animal behavior is animal behavior and *human* **behavior** is *human* **behavior**.

Chapter 4

Rewards Stunt Growth of Intrinsic Motivation

This leads me to this whole idea of rewards—I touched on behavioral plans and the behavioral side, but I didn't talk about rewards systems and **why** they **don't work so well**.

The answer boils down to two reasons. The first reason why rewards **don't work** is because adults who use them are operating under the assumption they are **mind readers**; that a parent can actually figure out what motivates his or her son/daughter to do something.

Truth be told, it is **nearly impossible** to figure out what **actually motivates** a child to do something. A child does what he/she does for a **variety** of reasons, and it is usually **about the child**.

So in cases where adults "know for sure" their child thinks TV is the best reward, or they know spending extra time with friends on the weekend is what will motivate their child to do better in school, the truth is adults **don't** have the ability to know. It's actually a lot of **guess work,** and I don't like guess work.

I like to know what I'm up against, and I like to figure out a plan based on as much input from a child as possible. I don't want to be guessing what motivates a child. I want the child to tell me.

The second reason why rewards don't work is because, as a society, we have become really crazy about rewarding *everything;* Adults even try to reward **activities of daily living**—the activities people do to stay alive.

Activities of daily living (i.e., getting up, getting dressed, cleaning ourselves, feeding ourselves) have become targets for parents to reward because these are activities that most children **don't** like to do.

We've reached a point where a reward has to be given for doing the things that keep us alive. That is absurd to me. A child should not have the opportunity to get fifty points for brushing teeth and then save up points to get candy or a toy later. You see, the point of brushing teeth is so the child can **keep** his/her teeth.

Another example is eating; some parents will tell their child, "If you stay at the table and eat your dinner, you can see a movie on Friday."

I don't know what that has to do with eating and **staying alive**, but somehow we have this **crazy idea** that if we just **bribe** a child, we can get the child to do the things the child is supposed to do for the sake of doing it. That is really absurd to me.

Like I said earlier, brushing your teeth is to keep your teeth, eating your food is mandatory for survival. I think when adults say "rewards" they are really using **bribes**.

Because parents are not taught how to **motivate** their child, they begin to guess. Adults say, "I think my son will like that; he has tons of Batman toys. So if I offer to get him a Batman game, he'll start listening every time I ask him to do something." Unfortunately, getting your child to listen **doesn't** work that way.

Chapter 5
Parent as Leader

Individuals play many roles throughout their lives. Some roles involve interacting with people that are above you:

>Parents
>Grandparents
>Teachers
>Employers
>Law enforcement

Other roles involve interacting with people that are below you:

>Children
>Grandchildren
>Students
>Employees
>Citizens

Finally, we have roles when interacting with people on the same level:

> Friends
> Lovers
> Siblings
> Classmates
> Co-workers
> Colleagues

What gets **confusing** is when an individual becomes a parent, he or she interacts with others on **all three levels,** *simultaneously*!

Parents have to balance their personal identity because the majority of their lives have been spent formulating relationships with others **as equals** or listening to individuals **above** them.

A new parent can be extremely challenged and unsure of how to handle his or her **emerging** role as superior when a child is born. After all, this newborn is the sole responsibility of the two new parents. Questions are bound to arise concerning how to **define** and **balance** this unfamiliar role we call parenting.

Defining the role of parent

Although children come through parents, they are **not** extensions of parents. They are **selfish** from birth to ensure *their* **survival**, and the things they say and do are about them. They will continue to act this way until their current problem-solving strategies are replaced with socially accepted ones. Therefore, **defining** the role of parent is simply **leading** them.

Successful leadership is achieved by teaching your child socially acceptable skills that will help him or her transition from childhood to adulthood. By making this investment, he or she can carry on the **family legacy** and become **productive** members of society.

Balancing the role as parent

When it comes to balancing the role as parent, consider the following. To take care of your child, you must **first** take care of yourself. Many parents ignore this rule, and they quickly become exhausted because they do not take care of themselves.

Secondly, if you are co-parenting, it is best to model a healthy relationship by putting that relationship first. This will provide a blueprint for all of the child's future relationships with people, on all three levels of interaction. Sometimes parents will disagree; however, it's best to have a united front, whenever possible.

Thirdly, when you need support, guidance, or have questions, seek help from adults **on** your level or **above** your level. Too often children are bombarded with adult anxieties, worries, and responsibilities when it is not age-appropriate for their development.

Finally, have consistent rules and a set schedule for everyone. Make sure that the rules/schedules are clearly defined, predictable, and leave some room for flexibility. Ultimately, it is not a good idea to deviate too far from any set schedule.

The following chapters of this manual will explain in greater detail how to balance your role as leader. Although this role may be complicated at times, it is the most important, exciting, and fun investment any parent will ever have!

Chapter 6

Communication

What is communication? Communication is the way we humans send verbal, nonverbal (or both) messages from one person to another.

It is important to note the difference between the verbal messages we send to and from one another, and the nonverbal messages we send to and from one another. Let's examine the differences between the two.

Verbal communication is defined as the actual words people use to speak. You may or may not be aware of this, but verbal communication only makes up 10 percent of the messages we send to one another. In actuality, 90 percent of the messages we send back and forth require **no words at all!** This is called nonverbal communication.

Nonverbal communication is defined as sending messages back and forth to one another without words. These messages are sent to others through:

Eye contact
Facial expressions
Voice tone
Voice volume
Rate of speech
Silences/pauses
Hand gestures
Body positioning
Body distance

The most successful people on the planet have the ability to tap into the 90 percent of communication that really reaches and leads people. If I had the choice to understand and apply verbal communication skills vs. nonverbal communication skills, I would prefer the nonverbal!

Why? Because if communication (verbal and nonverbal) was given as a test, I would rather receive a 90 percent and get an A! How would you want to score?

Let us examine these nine powerful ways we send messages to one another as well as our children. With this new found knowledge, the current way you look at parenting your child will change forever!

I am about to show you how to tap into the nonverbal form of communication, so you can be aware of what is **really** going on around you.

<u>Eye contact</u>

Examine any fight, argument, or disagreement. What is the first thing that goes between two people?

Eye contact!

There is just no way around it. When someone doesn't want to talk about the same subject or doesn't want to do what another person is doing, he or she will look away immediately.

Why does this happen? In short, looking into another person's eyes is very **intimate** and **personal**. For some reason, it is **extremely** hard to look someone in the eye and be upset with the person at the same time.

You think you can look into someone's eyes and be upset with him or her for an extended period of time? Try it. The next time you are upset with your child, or anyone for that matter, make yourself look them in their eyes.

Notice if they are looking back. Monitor how long you both stare into each other's eyes before the negative feeling goes away.

I'd give it thirty seconds to one minute tops! You won't be able to help feeling reconnected with them, just through eye contact.

How can you use this nonverbal tool to your advantage? Simply look at your child to see if he or she is still looking at you. (Long before they tantrum or become extremely difficult, they will look away). Use this as an indicator of their current state and to re-establish a connection with them, by initiating eye contact.

Facial expressions

Just like eye contact, facial expressions are powerful ways to communicate nonverbally! In fact, even if your child is not making eye contact, you still have the ability to be "in tune" with him or her by looking at the child's facial expressions.

This is because whether children are happy, sad, angry, afraid, excited, frustrated, embarrassed, surprised, worried, jealous, disappointed, hurt, sorry, ashamed, proud, enraged, interested, disgusted, joyous, or in awe, it is **almost impossible** to completely mask how they feel during that moment.

How do you use this nonverbal tool to your advantage? Simply stop what you are doing, and take the time to look at their facial expressions.

As you do this, do not try to change their feelings, simply voice what you see ("You look angry"). This will encourage them to talk with you instead of continuing to stay quiet or closed off emotionally.

Voice tone

Voice tone is an interesting way to communicate nonverbal messages to others, because you can make one statement and the statement can have several meanings. This is achieved by the words you choose to **emphasize** with your tone of voice.

Voice tone communicates nonverbally how a person feels emotionally (happy, sad, angry, afraid, excited, frustrated, embarrassed, surprised, worried, jealous, disappointed, hurt, sorry, ashamed, proud, enraged, interested, disgusted, joyful, and awed). Voice tone can also communicate nonverbally what a person **thinks** about something, and what they plan to **do** about it.

How do you use this nonverbal tool to your advantage? By monitoring your own tone of voice, and stating your words as matter-of-factly as possible, you will be teaching your children how to be **calm, cool, and collected** when things don't go their way.

Communication

Voice volume

Voice volume is another interesting way to communicate nonverbal messages to others because it communicates that we were **not heard** or **understood**. We are repeating ourselves in a louder volume to be heard!

Usually a person will have a louder voice volume if he or she doesn't **feel heard**, or if he or she was **purposefully ignored**.

Voice volume communicates nonverbally how a person feels emotionally. It especially communicates excitement, happiness, anger, frustration, rage, jealousy, pride, or disgust with others. Voice volume is also used as a power move to interrupt or control other people, by talking over them.

How do you use this nonverbal tool to your advantage? By monitoring your own voice volume and speaking lower, others will follow. Remember, it takes two people to have a shouting match. Simply, the next time your children (or anyone) are yelling at you, deliberately lower your voice, and watch how long it takes for them to stop shouting. I'd give it thirty seconds, and they will follow your lead.

Rate of speech

Rate of speech is defined as how fast or how slowly a person speaks to another. Rate of speech can communicate nonverbally either **in-depth knowledge** or **pure uncertainty** about any subject matter. It can also communicate nonverbally the **patience** or **impatience** the speaker has with the person listening.

When a person knows the ins and outs of a particular topic, he or she may have an **increased** rate of speech because he or she has mastered that subject matter. The person is not tripping over his or her words because he or she has sufficient practice and expertise.

On the other hand, someone may speak extremely fast to act as if he or she has such mastery; but when you take a closer look, the person really doesn't. The person is simply talking fast to hide his or her uncertainty from the listener (or he/she is nervous).

When a person knows the ins and outs of a particular topic, he or she may have a **decreased** rate of speech because the person has mastered that subject matter. He or she is purposefully speaking slower so the listener can process the material.

On the other hand, this is not always the case. Sometimes the speaker will talk slowly because he or she does not know the material enough, and the person is searching for the right words to say.

Finally, rate of speech communicates nonverbally that the speaker has time to talk (communicating patience) or doesn't have time to talk (communicating impatience). When this happens the speaker can lead the conversation in a way that can leave the listener feeling great or absolutely horrible about himself or herself.

How do you use this nonverbal tool to your advantage? By monitoring the rate of speech, you will be making sure the listener has an inviting environment to **truly** listen. Listeners want to feel like they can be there for the speaker and contribute to a conversation. If you would like to build a strong connection between yourself and your child, it is important to monitor how fast/slow you speak.

Silences/pauses

Without a door we would never be able to leave a room. It is the *space* that is *cut out* of a room that gives us the ability to go inside/outside the room. We call this space a door.

Communication

Without a window we would never be able to feel the weather outside. It is the *space* that is *cut out* of a wall that lets fresh air in/out of the room. We call this space a window.

Without a period in a sentence, we would never be able to read. It is the *space* that is *cut out* of a sentence that gives us the ability to read and write. We call this space a period.

Finally, without silences/pauses we would never be able to communicate (verbally or nonverbally) with others. It is the *space* that is *cut out* of communication that helps structure all the verbal and nonverbal messages we send out and receive from others. We call this space a silence/pause.

Silences/pauses are a necessary part of communicating verbally and nonverbally with others. A buffer of time is needed between the messages you send to your child, and a pause so he or she can receive the information.

If you are sending **rapid fire** messages without any pauses, you are not giving the child a chance to understand or act accordingly.

How do you use this nonverbal tool? First, know that a relationship can grow in only two directions: **together** or **apart**. When you use silence the way it is **intended**, you will help your relationship **grow with** your child.

On the other hand, constantly sending verbal and nonverbal messages of discontent (without any pauses) will cause your relationship to **grow apart**.

So the next time you are giving a direction to your children, **stop** and give them a chance to process what you said. Wait quietly, and watch them do what you asked them to do. Also, when you are explaining your thoughts/feelings to them, **stop** after two or three sentences and check-in to see if they understand your statements.

Ask them, "What do you hear me saying?" or "What did I ask you to do?" Wait **silently** for them to answer completely. You will be surprised to find out that 85 percent of the time, what they heard was not your intended message.

Calmly restate the part of the message they did not understand. Also, give your children a chance to ask a question, or make a relevant comment when appropriate.

Body language (hand gestures and body positioning)

From the time we were born, body language (hand gestures and body positioning) was our first form of communicating with others. For the first **two–three years** of our life, we literally **did not have the words,** so our bodies "spoke" for us. We rapidly learned how to use our bodies to speak because our lives depended on it.

Even now we know how to speak and formulate sentences, but our body language is still the first signal we send out to other people. Pay attention when someone is speaking, and you will literally **see** that his or her body language speaks several seconds **before** words are vocalized!

As a rule of thumb, whatever the mouth does not **verbalize**, the body will say **physically**. Not only that, but even when the mouth does speak, our bodies will still **supplement** the words with body movements, bringing to life our unique form of self-expression.

When we use hand gestures, we are really putting the words we say into **action**. This serves as **a necessary** and **dramatic affect** that **emphasizes** our communication and current emotional state.

How do you use this nonverbal tool to your advantage? First, start to pay more attention and look at your child's body movements. As you practice this task, you will soon be able to see that you will know what he or she is trying to say verbally (sometimes before the child). Their body will speak first, as they think and search in their word bank for the most effective words to say in that moment.

As you are able to know where the child is going and follow his or her story, a strong connection will be established between you and your child. Your child (or anyone else) can have no better feeling because being in tune with him or her is one of the basic human needs. Paying attention to body language is the fastest and most efficient way to understand and connect with your child.

Body Distance

Body distance is the last tool to examine in nonverbal communication. Simply put, body distance is used to take over someone's personal space or give someone personal space. When we are really close to someone physically, it communicates care, concern, seriousness, or someone's safety is in jeopardy. When we are far away from someone physically, it communicates less care, less concern, relaxation, and freedom is permitted.

Usually we see two types of children: those that need their personal space **invaded** for them to calm down, self-regulate, or do what you ask them to do; and those that need **extra space** for them to calm down, self-regulate, and do what you ask them to do. Experiment with both to find the particular balance your child has. Sometimes you will need to move closer, and other times you will need to move away.

How do you use this nonverbal tool to your advantage? When you are asking your children to do something and they just are not moving, test and see which type of children they are. If they are the "I won't do it till someone is on me" type, **move closer** (regardless of age).

Note: As a last resort, only use force that is necessary to get the child to move. Lashing out physically is not needed to get your child to do what you ask him or her to do. If you do lash out, just remember you are teaching your children how to deal with people **smaller** and **weaker** than them…with smaller people **they'll do the same!**

Making them **do it** will communicate you are serious in that moment. They know you care, even if you are on top of them making them do something they don't want to do.

You are not killing them, like they will try to convince you. The mess will be cleaned in a minute or two, they will forget about it, and they'll go back to playing.

If you find that your children are the "give me fifteen seconds and I'll do it by myself" type, and no danger is involved, **move away**. (Or if talking to your children is making them more upset, you can move and use silence!).

Even when they tantrum, you can still give them space. Just remember it is **their** loss of control, **not yours**. As fast as they upset themselves, they can **calm themselves down!**

When they are **calmer**, come back. They know you care about them when you are far away. They just want what they want, and they want it *now*! There is no need to apologize because you let them be for two minutes.

Putting it all together

This is probably one of the first introductions you have been exposed to with such an **in-depth** look at nonverbal communication. Even though it can be a lot to process, **take your time with it**.

Avoid trying to lump all nine tools together at once or you will frustrate yourself. You will experience a noticeable shift in the dynamics between you and your child by combining two or maybe three of these nonverbal techniques.

With these new tools under your belt, power, flexibility, and leadership skills will be transferred back to where they are supposed to be—**in your hands!**

Chapter 7
Needs vs. Wants

With a better understanding of verbal and nonverbal communication, let us examine the difference between a child's needs and a child's wants. Is there a difference? Yes, there is a very big difference! I would like to take a moment to contrast the two. Let's take a closer look at these concepts.

When we say that a child **needs** something, what we are really talking about is a ...

>Necessary
>Element or
>Else
>Death

Sound drastic? It is supposed to be! This is because the needed "element" is the difference between life and death for that child! Here is a list of a child's needs. (Most of them you'll know):

- **Food:** grains, meats and beans, fruits, vegetables, milk, fats, oils, and sweets (sparingly on the last three);

- **Water:** 70 percent of our body is water; it is vital for survival;
- **Shelter:** to protect us from climate and weather changes;
- **Structure:** routines, predictability, and to bring order to a world that can be chaotic at times;
- **Unconditional Acceptance** (to belong): others are in tune with us as we communicate (Like a radio station, we need others to pick up on our "frequency" for survival.);
- **Belief in Something:** religions, science, rituals, etc.;
- **Clothing:** depends on the climate where you live.

When we say that a child **wants** something, what we are really saying is that:

> **W**ishes that
> **A**re
> **N**ice
> **T**o have
> **S**ometimes

Not so drastic? Exactly! This is because children's wants are the wish list that they can really *live without*. As for a list of a child's wants, simply include everything **off** the needs list! How can parents balance wants vs. needs? We need to provide all needs and leverage all the wants. (We will discuss later what leverage is and how to use it).

But like I said earlier, I really want to look more closely at these concepts. With a deeper look, we will see even *needs* have a deceptive quality about them, and they can become *wants*.

- **Food:** candy bars, fried chicken, cakes, chips, fast food;
- **Water:** Hi C, soda, milk shakes, sweetened ice tea, etc.;
- **Shelter:** an eight-bedroom, four-bathroom, three-car garage (when it is only for two people) home;

- **Structure:** minute by minute plan for each day or no plan for each day;
- **Unconditional Acceptance:** everyone has to agree with us or like us. Everyone must be our friend;
- **Belief in Something:** Christianity, Judaism, or Hinduism is the "only way of life" and all others will **suffer;**
- **Clothing:** top of the line, name-brand clothing, shoes, etc.

Throughout the history of man, children have always "wanted what they want, and they want it **now!**" This is not a new invention created by this generation of children. In fact, this is the way children have always reacted **in all generations**. Children act this way because they are **selfish**. In the beginning stages of life, this selfishness is **necessary** for their survival.

How can a child's selfishness be necessary for survival? If children were not selfish, they would not cry when they were hungry, thirsty, or needed a diaper change. Without these "selfish" cries, the parent would never know what the child needed, and the child would **die**.

Unfortunately, parents have not been exposed to this information; plus, with technological advancements, basic human needs have been changed into wants (as shown in the section above).

For example, when we were a farming society, did crops grow overnight? No, the family was forced to wait until they were ripe.

As the family waited, parents did not sulk, feel like bad parents, or let their children convince them they were horrible providers because the corn wasn't ready fast enough.

In fact, tantrums would be a useless strategy for children because hysterical crying would not speed up the process. The crops were ready when they were ready.

With great technological advancements, society has drastically changed. In today's world we can actually get what we want and get it **now**, whatever "it" may be. We do not have to wait five months for crops to grow.

In fact, with the invention of fast-food restaurants, we do not have to wait more than **five minutes,** and the food is ready! On top of that, there are so many places to choose from, and they are all within a short distance!

Don't get me wrong; technological advancements have been **wonderful** tools for the human race. These advancements have helped us run operations faster, more smoothly, and more efficiently than ever before!

But bad always comes with the good, and in many respects our technological advancements have played a big role in the breakdown of parent-child and family dynamics. Children want it now, and parents want their children in control now. This is a recipe for disaster.

What can parents do to solve this confusion between a child's needs vs. a child's wants? Simply, parents must **provide all** needs, and **leverage all** wants.

How do I leverage my child's wants? Using leverage is like using a car jack. A car jack physically moves the car upwards for us because we cannot lift a car. We push the lever up and down until the car slowly rises.

A child's outburst is like the car, and his or her wants are like the lever to a car jack. We can literally **move** the difficult outburst in the direction **we lead** by using his or her wants as a tool for us. How do we achieve this?

First, be aware that you might feel sorry, embarrassed, or frustrated because you stood your ground. The child will work hard to change your mind. When they try to convince you that their wants are truly a need, simply remember that you are still a caring and concerned parent, whether they get what they **want** or not. This is true 100 percent of the time! Also, remember the material thing is something they can **work for to earn in the future**.

Secondly, you can talk with your children about what they wanted even if they are absolutely not going to get it! Where age appropriate you can ask questions about the toy or whatever the desired thing was. You may learn something about your children that you did not know about them as you talk about it. This will help you to be in tune with them—a real need— and open the door for future communication between you and your child.

Finally, if your attempts at talking about it don't work, remain calm. Your child has a shorter attention span than you do! You can always change the subject; tell your child to help you with something (to distract), or simply say, "I'm not talking about the ___ (fill in the blank) anymore" and remain **silent/calm**.

Since words were not working, **stop using them** for the time being. Everything will be okay, and you guys can talk again at a later time (usually in just minutes). Ultimately your child will be learning how to deal with **authority** and develop **coping skills** based on what *you say/do*. You must remain calm, cool, and collected as much as possible, or else he or she will just follow your out-of-control lead in the future.

Chapter 8
How Children Learn

After examining the difference between what a child needs vs. what a child wants, let's discuss how children learn. Children learn:

Through the **multiple pairing** of the five senses
By **trial** and **error**
By **feedback** from others
Deliberate practice

Now that we know how children learn *all things*, let's take a moment to define the difference between **academic** learning and **social** learning.

Academic learning (reading, writing, arithmetic):
Teaches students how to speak grammatically correct, read, write, add, subtract, multiply, and divide.

Social learning (how to be a human being):
Teaches students how to follow directions, cooperate with others, share, make friends, initiate/maintain conversations,

empathize, self-regulate (physically and emotionally), and to be aware of social cues.

The teaching profession has known for a long time the best ways to create an environment for academic learning. For some odd reason, these wonderful strategies go out the window when it comes to teaching children social, emotional and/or behavioral skills. What strategies do teachers use during an academic lesson?

The following example will help you learn a systematic approach when teaching algebra to others.

1) Instructor has to know how to solve the problem **before** they are **allowed** to teach it.

> Example: an eighth grade algebra teacher is certified to teach eighth grade algebra.

> (Unless proper certification was received, an eighth grade math teacher would not be qualified to teach twelfth grade calculus)

2) Instructions are provided in a manner that tells students **what** to do.

> Example: "Your homework for tonight will be questions one through fifteen on page seven."

> Instructions tell students **how** they can do it (In **chronological order** and framed in the positive.)

> During class a teacher may say, "To solve the equation $3x - 6 = 18$ you must…

First, isolate the variable by adding 6 to both sides;
Second, divide by 3 on both sides;
Third, you will have the answer to this equation;
Finally, check your answer by plugging in the variable. Use the order of operations (x, /, +, -) to help check answer."

3) Instructions will use **multiple senses** (seeing, hearing, touching, tasting, smelling) to teach students.

- The student will **see** the steps written out on the chalk board;
- The student will **touch** the pencil and feel the motion of writing the numbers on paper;
- The student will **hear** the words.

$$3x - 6 = 18$$
(First) $\quad +6 \quad +6$

$$\underline{3x} = \underline{24}$$
(Second) $\quad 3 \quad\quad 3$

(Third) $\quad X = 8$

(Final check) $3(8) - 6 = 18$
(Order of Operations) $3 \times 8 = 24$

(8 is the Correct answer) $24 - 6 = 18$

(These steps will solve any **algebraic** equation.)

4) Correct responses are reinforced **without** too much emotion (a check, sticker, smiley face, "great job on #3," an A, etc.)

5) Multiple equations are given to **deliberately practice** the newly learned skill (quizzes and tests serve same purpose)

Combining steps one through five will teach a child any *academic* **lesson.**

In a nutshell, here is the system and strategy teachers use to teach their students.

- The **teacher** has to know **how** to **solve** the problem;
- The teacher has to give directions telling a student **what to do** and **how to it** (in **chronological order** and **stated** in the *positive*);
- The material is paired with *multiple* **senses**, so the student can begin solving the problem;
- Through **trial and error**, the student (as the experimenter) uses his or her abilities to process the information, and the student continues to solve the problem;
- **Feedback** is given from the teacher to show the student what **is** working and what **is not** working;
- More **deliberate** practice is given until they are able to master solving the problem.

Interestingly enough, if you look at this list **closely**, you will see that five out of the six steps involve the *teacher's ability to present* and *structure* the material. In other words about 85 percent of the student's learning is completely **outside of a student's ability to control.**

Remember the algebraic equation earlier? Let's examine what a teacher would do if the student did the following:

Let's say, **instead** of doing this—

$$3x - 6 = 18$$
(First) $\quad +6 \quad +6$

(Second) $\quad \dfrac{3x}{3} = \dfrac{24}{3}$

(Third) $\quad x = 8$

(Final check) $3(8) - 6 = 18$

The student **does**—

(First) $\quad \dfrac{3x - 6 = 18}{3 \qquad\qquad 3}$

(Second) $\quad x - 6 = 6$
$\quad\quad\quad\quad +6 \ +6$

(Third) $\quad x = 12$

What are the **two** mistakes the student made?

1) The student was supposed to isolate the variable by adding 6 to both sides **first**. Instead, this student divided by 3.

2) The student **did not check** his/her answer. If he or she did, the student would have noticed that $12 \times 3 = 36$… and…$36 - 6 = 30$ (Clearly, 12 is the **wrong** answer)

So what do teachers do when a child is having trouble in an **academic** subject? Teachers have a totally different mindset and approach when students are struggling academically. The mindset and strategies include the following:

With **infrequent** academic problems, teachers handle it by

- Believing the student is **trying to do it correctly**;
- Believing the student made a mistake **by accident**;
- Giving the student **more** examples to **practice**;
- Believing they will be **successful** at it in the future.

When the student is having **chronic** academic problems, they

- Believe the student **accidentally learned it wrong**;
- **Identify** where the student **misunderstood**;
- **Present the information** differently to the student;
- Focus on the basic **rules** or **foundation** of material;
- Provide **appropriate feedback**;
- Give **more examples to practice**;
- Believe they will be **successful** at it in the future;

As I mentioned earlier, for some **odd** reason, these excellent strategies are ignored when it comes to teaching children social, emotional, and behavioral skills. Instead, children are viewed as:

- Not caring;
- Being "bad";
- Being "evil";
- Being lazy;
- Not trying hard enough;
- Having a "character flaw";
- Not living up to his/her potential.

This is simply not true! The reality is children are **separate** from their actions, and they are **wonderful** just as they are.

They simply lack the appropriate **social, emotional and/or behavioral skills** in *certain* socially challenging situations.

Once the material is presented in a **new** way, **deliberately practiced**, and the **correct feedback** is given, they will **change** their inappropriate behaviors. The following formula shows your role in the process.

The Mind-Shift (You)

+

New Presentation (You)

+

Deliberate Practice (You and Child)

+

Proper Feedback (You)

+

(More Deliberate Practice & Proper Feedback over Time)

=

Appropriate Social Skill (Child)

When it comes down to it, learning how to follow directions, cooperate with others, share, make friends, initiate/maintain conversations, empathize with others as well as how to pick up on social cues are skills that are **learnable** and **teachable**.

We don't need to re-invent the wheel because academic teaching has already given us a road map to successfully teach social learning.

The next chapter will provide tools for the proper **mindset** to have **before** learning how to effectively give directions. With this mind shift, you will walk away with a new understanding and become the **best** social, emotional, and behavioral teacher your children will ever have in their lives!

Chapter 9
The Mind Shift (Your Job)

The **mindset** of giving effective directions to a child is the same mindset of planning a vacation. What is the very first step in planning a vacation?

You have to know where you want to go!

In other words you must pick a destination **before** you can plan the length of the trip, the hotel stay, the flight plans, and clothes you are going to bring.

The same knowing is crucial when giving directions to your children; you must know **what you want** from them and **where you want** the interaction to go **before** they can follow directions.

How can this be applied in **real** life? Let's say that you walk into your child's room, and you see a "disaster." First, realize that every person has a different definition of "clean" vs. "dirty."

Because different people have different **thresholds** of cleanliness, the proper *mindset* would be to ask *yourself* the following *before* directing your child:

- When this room is clean, how do **I want** it to look?
- Where do **I want** his or her toys to be?
- Where do **I want** his or her dirty cloths to be?
- What do **I want** my child to do with the toys under the bed?
- What do **I think** is a clear and neat desk?

Now why in the world would I ask myself all these questions about the *child's* room? Again we are focused on the mindset. Your mindset is to know what you want **before** you direct your child, so he or she can complete any task. So the first step in shifting your mindset is to literally get out a piece of paper and ask yourself the above questions.

Whether you write down your answers or not doesn't really matter. However, writing it down will make things **clearer** for the both of you. With clear written instructions, both you and your child will be able to see **exactly** what your expectations are.

The beauty of this assignment is that it **doesn't matter** how neat you want the room to be! You are the parent, and the room needs to look however you see fit. You just can't expect your child to carry out your vision if it is not clearly defined.

Here are some more examples of common questions to ask yourself before you give your child directions.

They include the following:

- How do I want my bedtime routine to go with my children?
- How do I want my morning routines to go with my children?

- How do I want bath time routines to go?
- How do I want my children to act during meal times?
- How loud do I want the volume in the house to be?
- How do I want my children to get along when they play?
- How do I want my weekends to go?
- What do I want my children to do while shopping?
- What do I want my children to do during car rides?
- What time do I want homework started?
- What time do I want homework finished?
- What do I consider a pleasant dinner time with the family?
- What do I consider "good" manners?
- What is a "nice" time at the park with the children?
- Where is the appropriate place for the children to run?

The bottom line: this list is just the tip of the iceberg. You can apply this mindset to **every** situation. Just know (and this is a guarantee) that if you have not clearly defined your expectations, your child will never be able to follow the direction.

Only by focusing on what you **do want** and *clearly* **defining your expectations** will your child meet your expectations.

If you find yourself thinking about and/or listing all of the things you **do not** want your child to do, **dig deeper**! Having a clear definition of what you **do not** want keeps the problem **alive**.

If you would like to **solve** the problem **in a useful way**, shift your list of "don't wants" and convert them into "do wants." How do you do that?

Examples of changing "Don't Wants" into "Do Want"

I don't want my child to run in the house.

becomes...

I want my child to run in the back yard.

I don't want my child to interrupt me when I'm talking.

becomes...

I want my child to say "excuse me" when I'm talking to others.

I don't want my child taking things out of the refrigerator alone.

becomes...

I want my child to ask for an apple before he/she takes one.

I don't want my child to talk back when I ask him/her to clean up.

becomes...

I want my child to clean up quietly.

I don't want my child to talk so loud at the dinner table.

becomes...

I want a lower volume at the dinner table.

I don't want my child talk back when I ask him/her to do something.

becomes...

I want my child to following directions quietly.

The Mind Shift (Your Job)

Why do this? When you focus on what you want and have a clear, well-defined goal, you will be able to take the steps to achieve that goal. Goal-setting applies to every aspect of your entire life! Giving effective directions **starts** by knowing where you want to go **before** changes can be made to meet your expectations.

The last and probably most important step in the **mind-shift** is to **assume** the **best** in your child's **intent** and/or **motivation**. Nine times out of ten parents decide that the only purpose or motivation behind a child's action is to:

> Hurt
> Harm
> Attack
> Annoy
> Bother
> Disrupt
> Frustrate

*Look closer...this is usually **not** the case*

Nine times out of ten the child's intention, motivation, or purpose was none of the above! Instead, the **result** of their behavior is due to a lack of a learnable or teachable **social skill**!

It's really time to make a mind-shift that views your child's intentions **as good**! Not only that, but one that also views the child as doing **his or his best,** given their developmental, social, and/or emotional state during that moment.

Instead of viewing their actions as a personal attack, shift to viewing your child as a **great child** that made an **inappropriate action or comment.** Just this one change in parental attitude can rebuild any damaged parent-child relationship.

So the next time you observe your child (even when he or she makes an obvious mistake), **assume** his or her motives were **positive**. Dig deep enough you will always find a motivation that promotes pro-social behaviors! The best gift you can give to the relationship between you and your child is to **assume the best in your child**. Focus your energies on catching him or her "doing right" instead of "doing wrong."

Chapter 10

The New Presentation (Your Job)

In the previous chapter, we went over the mistakes that parents make **before** giving directions (not knowing **what they want** and **assuming the worst**).

Now let us examine other common mistakes that parents make when **verbally stating directions** to their children. These common mistakes include the following:

1) **Improper m*odeling*** by parents;
2) **Asking** instead of telling;
3) Giving **too many** *choices*/Giving **no choice** at all;
4) **Reasoning** with child;
5) **Expecting** a transition **without** any warning;
6) Parents **verbally state** what they **don't want**;
7) Directions lack **chronological order** and do **not** have a **clear** beginning, middle, and end to a task;
8) Giving **too many directions** at one time;
9) **Personal commentaries** mixed in with directions;
10) **Begging/pleading/bribing**…instead of leverage;

1) Improper modeling by parents

It is important to stress that it would be an excellent idea for parents to **say** and **do** the things **they expect** from their children. Yes parents "call the shots"; yet children can follow your lead much easier **if you do what you expect from them, as well.**

For example, if you expect your children to say "please" and "thank you," they will learn it (and apply it) much faster if **you say** "please" and "thank you" **whenever possible.**

One of the most common mistakes is the parent that *yells* at the child for *yelling* in the house; or the parent that *hits* the child for *hitting* his or her younger brother or sister.

It sounds silly; yet this is a very **common** practice by **many** parents. When this happens the nonverbal message sent to children is "do as I say and not as I do." If you would like your children to act appropriately when they are frustrated, it is vital that you **model** that behavior when you are frustrated. Modeling behaviors to children is essential in their learning process.

2) Asking instead of telling

Many times parents are not aware that when asking their children to do something they are **really** attempting to **tell** them what to do. It is usually disguised by the misuse of your **tone of voice** (specifically, by putting it in a question form, instead of a command form).

Examples:
"Are you ready for bed?"
(When it is past bed time)
"Can you put on you coat, please?"

(When the child is outside in the cold)
"Would you like to take a bath now?"
(When it's bath time)
"Could you come to the table to eat with us?"
(When it's dinner time)
"Why won't you sit still?"
(When you want them to stop moving)
"Why aren't you dressed yet?"
(When school starts in five minutes)

Anytime a question is being presented to children, the question communicates **nonverbally** that they have **some say** in the matter.

If in that moment they do not want to do something (or don't feel like it), they will avoid it! Your child "appears" defiant because of the illusion of a choice that **did not exist**.

Let us now discuss how to turn those questions into **calm, yet firm** commands. It is important to have a **neutral** tone of voice because it shows your child that you are standing your ground. Also, your calmness is **contagious** and will help your child calm down.

Are you ready for bed? (When it is past bed time)

becomes...

It's bed time.

Can you put on your coat, please? (When the child is outside)

becomes...

It is cold outside, put your coat on.

Would you like to take a bath now?" (When it's bath time)

becomes...

It's bath time.

Could you come to the table to eat with us? (When it's dinner time)

becomes...

It's dinner time; come sit at the table with us.

(Please note that **an action must** be accompanied with these new ways of **calmly** stating your directions. Words alone are empty because they only make up 10 percent of communication; a nonverbal follow-through must back up the words. We will discuss how to **follow through** in **Chapter 11**)

3) <u>Giving too many choices/giving no choice at all</u>

I want to finally demystify this whole idea of giving choices to your child/teen. Too many choices and your child/teen will become **overwhelmed by having to pick**. Not enough choices and your child will feel like he or she **has "no say at all,"** and the child **will rebel**. So what is the solution?

Give two choices that you are perfectly okay with no matter what he or she picks. Do your best to pick two choices that will **balance** what he/she is **allowed to do** with what the child would **enjoy** doing.

Example: "It is bed time...would you like to walk holding hands or have a piggy-back ride?"

If the child gives an alternative that will help accomplish the intended goal (of getting to bed), **use** his/her idea, even if it was not a part of the original choice.

Example: "It is bed time...would you like to walk holding hands or have a piggy-back ride?"

Child asks, "Can we march?"

(Go with it!)

This is clearly a child that is cooperating and has thought of a different/creative way to get to the bed. Allow this to happen!

If the child does not work with you and gives an unacceptable alternative, calmly restate what time it is and repeat the choices (in a shortened version).

Example: "It is bed time...would you like to walk holding hands or go for a piggy-back ride?"

Child says, "I want play outside."

"Tomorrow you can play outside. Right now it is bed time. Hold hands or piggy-back ride?"

If the child still does not want to cooperate and his or her alternative is out of the question, **calmly** state that he or she has ten seconds to decide, or you will choose. Count for real. Don't be invested if he/she decides in ten seconds or not; it is **the child's responsibility.** Follow through if ten seconds have passed, and the child has still not decided.

Example: "It is bed time...would you like to walk holding hands or have a piggy-back ride?"

Child says, "I want play outside"

"Tomorrow you can play outside. Right now it is bed time. Hold hands or piggy-back ride?"

Child says, "I don't want to go to bed!"

"I'll give you ten seconds to decide...if you don't choose, I will choose for you...ten...nine...eight..."

(Usually they will decide before you get to zero)

Then say, "Thank you for picking one"

In some cases the child may not make a decision. If so, choose for the child by taking his or her hand. If the child tries to fight it or throw himself/herself on the ground, **calmly** pick the child up and bring him/her to bed (**without** talking).

If he or she leaves the bed or comes out of the room, silently bring the child back to bed. The key is to stay **calm** because your calmness is contagious and will help your child calm down.

4) Reasoning with your child

In a perfect world, reasoning with your child would settle **all** debates, arguments, fights, shouting matches, and hurt feelings when your child doesn't get his/her way! Logically it would make total sense. If I simply explain to my child and give an acceptable reason, then he or she will "see the light."

The New Presentation (Your Job)

Then the child will transform his or her behavior and possibly even thank me for taking the time to explain it in such a caring and eloquently manner. Unfortunately this is not a perfect world—reasoning **while directing** simply is an **ineffective** parenting strategy.

It is wishful thinking for parents to give an explanation to their eight-year-old son as to why it is a bad idea to beat up his brother when the little brother stole a toy. Any conversation at this point will make the situation worse. In reality only a few ways are available to effectively handle these kinds of scenarios:

1) Stop any physical fighting immediately (only use force necessary to stop fight, not to hurt them);
2) Stay **neutral** from picking sides;
3) Review, reestablish, or create rules;
4) Provide verbal alternatives to physically fighting;
5) Have the child practice those alternatives right then and there;
6) Redirect interaction by reviewing rules or setting new rules for continuing play;
7) State consequences, if rules are not followed;
8) Follow through on consequences, if inappropriate behavior continues;
9) If follow-through is necessary, let the child know he or she will have another opportunity to try again the next day, when the child is able to follow directions.

Simply put, reasoning with your child while giving a direction is an ineffective leadership skill. In the majority of parent-child interactions, it is more effective to direct, redirect, instruct, give alternatives, set limits, provide consequences, and follow through.

When you can apply these strategies calmly and confidently, your child will be perfectly okay with being told what to do. When **you** are comfortable with giving directions **without a reason**, others will be comfortable **following your lead** without one too.

5) Expecting a transition without any warning

What is a transition? Transitions are the time period **right after one activity ends** and **just before a new activity begins**. In other words transitions are the period of time *in between* changing from one activity to the next. Depending on *how a transition is structured*, a transition can last seconds, minutes, hours, days, months, or even years!

Did you know that the most challenging human behaviors (defiance, arguments, tantrums, fighting, etc.) all occur **during** transitions? How does this happen? This happens because transitions have no rules, no structure, and people usually do not know what will happen next.

Let's take a moment to examine some major transitions we are presented with during our lives. These major **life transitions** include the following:

- Birth/death;
- Marriages/divorces;
- Starting/ending a job;
- Starting school/ending school;
- Moving (in/out of an apartment or home).

These major transitions bring to people some of their greatest joys as well as their greatest sorrows. Although how to handle these major life transitions are not the focus of this manual, they are extremely important to note.

The New Presentation (Your Job)

Now let's take a moment to examine the major transitions that occur daily. These major **daily** transitions include the following:

- Waking up/getting ready for day;
- Meal times;
- Bed time;
- Bath time;
- Leaving the house;
- Car rides;
- Coming home/evenings;
- Homework/household chores.

These transitional periods throughout the day can put a strain on any parent. That is why this section of the book is designed to help alleviate (even eliminate) challenging behaviors during these times.

Too often parents are not aware of these transition times, and they **expect** their child to **move** on a moment's notice. The most effective way to handle these transition times is by using the **10 minute, 5 minute, 1 minute, and then *Go* system**. The technique speaks for itself and would operate like this:

"(Child's Name), ten more minutes to...(the game, watch TV, etc.).

Then it is.... (bath time, bed time, dinner time, breakfast time, etc.)."

No other words needed in script

Set a timer for 10 minutes. When **5 minutes** remains, give your child another warning by saying:

"Five more minutes to (mention whatever they were doing)...

Then it is...(Fill in the blank time)."

No other words needed in script

When **1 minute** remains, give your child another warning by saying:

"It's ___ (fill in the blank) time in one minute."

(This is the time to tell the child to save his or her games, have one more turn down the slide at the park, one more turn before the board game ends, one more race before the child goes inside, pick one more thing to color, etc.)

No other words needed in script

When time is up...Move to the next thing...The child had plenty of warning, so this is not the time for three more turns or one more story before bed...This is the time to go!

Why is this so effective? This technique will help in two ways. One, your child will be given enough warning before it is time to switch, so he or she is **less likely** to rebel. Secondly, it teaches children how they can manage **their time wisely**.

If you are **consistent** with this approach during transitions, he or she will soon learn what to expect, how to experience time better, plan accordingly, and act out much less. But the child can only do so if the parent sticks to the 10, 5, 1, **and then** *Go* method.

One last note: Technology has given us a powerful tool to help with transitions. Usually television programs end on the half hour.

If your child happens to be watching TV, plan your transition times to **coincide with the natural ending** of the show or movie; this will make **transitions** tremendously easier.

6) <u>Parents verbally state what they **don't want**</u>

In the previous chapter, we discussed how most parents do not know what they do want **before** they lead the interaction. This common mistake occurs again, **as parents verbally direct** their child, in the moment.

In this section we will discuss how to give effective directions to your child by **telling** him/her **what to do** and **how to do it**.

A) *What to do…*

Typically, the first word that starts off *every* direction with a child is *don't…*

Don't run, don't play with your food, don't jump on the couch, don't talk back, don't take things without asking, don't chew gum in school, etc.

Please understand, this creates a **natural conflict** because…

It is **physically possible** to run, play with your food, jump on the couch, talk back, take things without asking, chew gum in school, and so on…

Therefore, to give effective directions, you must verbally state to your child **exactly** what he or she **is allowed to do**. This can be achieved by providing the child with one or maybe two acceptable alternatives to their inappropriate behavior/approach.

B) How to do it...

There are three ways to instruct your child/teen on how you want him/her to do a particular task. You can **verbally** describe how you want a task done. You can **show** him/her nonverbally.

Finally, you can do a **combination of both**, for better results. Here are some examples of what to say/do during some common scenarios.

1) Your child is jumping on the couch...

"Couches are for sitting on..."

(Then walk over and gently sit him/her down on the couch.)

2) Your child is bouncing a basketball in the house...

"A great place to bounce the ball is outside."

(Have the child bounce the ball outside, put it away, or take it away.)

3) Your child is standing on a chair to get cookies, without asking...

"If you would like to have a cookie, ask me first."

(Then walk over and gently take him/her off of the chair.)

4) As you read a story, your child will not stay still...

"I will continue reading when your body is still."

(Gently place his/her hands/feet where you want them to be.)

5) *Your six year old takes a toy from your twelve-year-old...*

"You need to ask to use his *DS*; give it back and ask."

You can follow up with...

"Five seconds to return the *DS*, or I will give it back"

6) *Your child is cleaning up and trying to carry too many dishes...*

"Carry the plate with two hands. Then come back for the cup."

7) *Your child is playing with their cereal instead of eating...*

"Spoons are for scooping the cereal."

(Show him/her how to hold the spoon and scoop the cereal)

Tons of these examples come up in our daily lives. Way too many to count! These examples demonstrate how to lead your child so he or she can succeed at following directions. Remember, children must have clear directions that explain **what to do** and **how to do it**.

7) Directions lack chronological order (have no clear beginning, middle, or end)

Every story, whether spoken, read, or watched in movie form, is structured with a clear beginning, middle, and end. Without this structure, it would not be *one* story. Instead, it would be a series of **random** and **isolated** situations **thrown together**. Too often parents do not realize they are providing their child with ineffective directions when they do not say what to do **first**, what to do **second**, what to do **third**, and what to do **last**.

Beginning...

Children need a clear starting point when given a direction. Without a beginning to the task, they will never finish. Often times this is where parents will reason with their children, and they believe this is step one in giving the direction. Unfortunately, it is not step one. Step one must be **clear** and **verbally stated**, so he or she will know where to begin.

Middle...

The middle section of a task occurs from **step two** and continues **until** the very **last step** is given. The middle is usually the hardest part to structure because this is where **all the work actually gets accomplished**. In the middle section, it is especially important to focus on telling the child **what to do** and **how to do it** in three steps or less.

End...

Just like all things in life must come to an end, so must directions. Usually parents do not know how to get their child to follow directions, so they figure if they just keep saying "oh, and one more thing..." their child will follow through on an infinite amount of tasks. After a while your child will notice that his/her tasks are a **bottomless pit** and he or she will start to resist **all requests**. That is why it is vitally important to structure all tasks in ways that have a **clear (and definite) endpoint!**

8) Giving too many directions at one time

The best way to give directions is to phrase it in the positive (telling the child what to do and how to do it) **in three steps or less**. What exactly is a "step"? A step is **one direction that breaks down an action into its simplest form.**

Here are some examples of a broken down, **one-step** direction. (All phrased in the positive, telling the child what to do and how to do it).

- Stand up;
- Lay down on your bed;
- Sit in the chair;
- Walk to the door.

Here are some examples of a broken down, **two-step** direction. (All phrased in the positive, telling the child what to do and how to do it).

- Stand up and walk to the door;
- Lie down on your bed and close your eyes;
- Sit in the chair and eat dinner;
- Walk to the door and wait there.

Here are some examples of a broken down, **three-step** direction. (All phrased in the positive, telling the child what to do and how to do it).

- Stand up, walk to the door, and open it;
- Lie down on your bed, close your eyes, and go to sleep;
- Sit in the chair, eat dinner, and then clean up;
- Walk to the door, wait there, and stand still.

These are clear-cut examples of breaking the action down into **its simplest form in three steps or less**. Most parents give a task "they believe" is one step; however, it **usually** involves **too many** steps. The reason why parents lump several steps together is because *parents* do them **automatically**.

Unfortunately for children, they have not gained enough mastery to do most skills independently. Here are some examples of directions parents give that they believe are stated in one step. **In actuality** these are directions **loaded with many steps.**

1) *"Get dressed"*: Getting dressed involves many elements. Putting on underwear, socks, pants, undershirt, t-shirts, long sleeves shirts, shoes (left vs. right), and (depending on the weather) gloves, hats, scarves, snow pants, etc.
(*On a cold winter day, getting dressed involves about ten steps!*)

2) *"Go to Sleep"*: Going to sleep involves more steps than meets the eye. One must calm himself/herself down, walk to bed, get in the bed, get adequate covering, lay still, close his/her eyes, remain still, get over the fear of being alone because the parent is going to leave, actually fall asleep, etc.

*Give the child some candy or drinks before bed and watch how "wired" he or she will be and how many times the child will be going in and out of the bathroom **before** calming down.*

3) *"Eat Your Food"*: Eating your food requires sitting in a chair calmly enough to…put his/her bottom in the chair, keep his/her legs straight, and reach the table…just to **get prepared** to eat.

(*That's about three–five steps **before** using **utensils**.*)

Then when the child is eating, he or she has to gain mastery of holding the utensil, stabbing the food, balancing the utensil (with food) to his/her mouth, and actually getting the food inside the mouth!

Finally, there is chewing the food without choking on it, and starting the process all over again.

*Eating your food, really takes **many** steps to accomplish.*

How can parents effectively handle these situations? Two effective ways are available to lead these situations. Structure these times by breaking these tasks down **into three steps (preferably one or two.)**

For example: It is morning time and everyone is getting ready for school. When it is time for him/her to get ready, instead of saying "get dressed," say...

1) "It is time to get dressed. (Hand the child his/her shirt and say) Put your shirt on (in a voice tone that is calm, cool, collected, and matter-of-fact)

Or if you like giving choices to your child, say...

2) "It is time to get dressed. (Show the child his/her shirt and pants) and say, "Shirt first or pants first?"

(Phrasing it this way communicates nonverbally that the child has **a choice** as to which **one** he/she wants to **put on first;** however, the child has **no choice** in **getting dressed!** As always use a tone of voice that is calm, cool, collected, and matter-of-fact.)

Then take two more articles of clothing and give two choices again. Repeat until your child is fully clothed.

In the beginning, breaking things down into steps will require effort on your part. As time goes on, you will automatically begin to feel comfortable breaking everything down into its simplest steps.

It will not only make your life **easier**; your child will do these things **independently** and **without resistance** once he/she can form the habit. Habits will only be formed once the child learns the daily routines are **broken down** and **predictable**.

9) <u>Personal commentaries mixed in with directions</u>

Every comment or spoken opinion **added into a direction counts as one extra step in that direction!** In other words if your child is running in the house and you say...

"Come on, Johnny... Stop running, and walk...we go through this every day...why did you do that?" (All stated in an agitated tone of voice.)

This "one" statement is loaded with more than three steps that send **contradictory messages**.

1) "Come on, Johnny" by itself is a command. However, the words used were not meant for him really to "come" or "go" anywhere.

2) "Stop running, and walk" is the heart of the message. However this does not tell the child/teen **what he/she can do** or **how to do it**.

3) "We go through this everyday" communicates the parent's frustration that **most** children would perceive themselves as "bad" or "no good" (especially when paired with an agitated tone of voice).

4) "Why did you do that?" invites little Johnny to believe that you are **actually asking him a question**. Depending on age, he will not be developed enough to understand this is a rhetorical question/statement.

If you remember from the previous section, we want our directions to be in **three steps or less**. Adding a commentary, put-down, an opinion, or voicing your personal frustration **while giving a direction** will create **an addition step** in the communication. Even though you may think you are only telling him "stop running," many **nonverbal** messages are **sub-communicated** when talking in this manner.

Adding personal commentaries is more than just adding too many steps. Even when **not intended**, they create additional information for your child/teen to process. Ultimately, commentaries are extraneous information **about you** and **your frustration**, and they are an adult version of "talking back." If you would like to give effective directions that your child will not resist, it is best to leave out the commentaries.

10) Begging/pleading/bribing…instead of using leverage

I firmly believe this last common mistake is a combination of the first *nine* **mistakes, all mixed together in a pot.** Sometimes begging, pleading, and bribing with a child can be a last resort.

In **most cases**, begging, pleading, and bribing are **a quick fix!** This is usually a **result of a balancing act** because parents:

Are responsible for their children's welfare/safety;
Have care, love, and concern for their children;
Are responsible for telling their children what to do;
Must have appropriate coping skills;
Must have appropriate problem solving skills;
Have not been taught **how** to leverage wants;
Want their children to "just do it already!"

Obviously **all** parents have love, care, and concern for their children, but **most of the time**, parents (as human beings) just want **their own** lives to run faster, smoother, and more efficiently. Just like children, parents want what **they want**, and **they want it now**.

So...

Of course you and your child/teen are going to "bump heads"... you are both using the **same strategy** to exert **power** over one another!

To get your **parental power** back, instead of begging **direct** the child; instead of pleading, **set limits**; and finally, instead of bribing, **follow through** with consequences.

By failing to **replace** the begging, pleading and bribing with these alternatives, you will be placing your child in the driver's seat of parent-child interactions.

The following chapters will provide an action plan to **prevent** this role reversal from becoming a permanent reality.

Chapter 11
Deliberate Practice

Children **say** and **do** the things that they do for **two reasons only**!

1) Because the things they **say** and **do work**!
2) Because they have **practiced** repeatedly!

"Good," "bad," "right," or "wrong," have **no bearing** on these two reasons. They are as true as any universal law, such as gravity. In fact, from this point forward, I will refer to this phenomenon as **reality communication**.

Reality communication is defined as the **actual outcome** of any parent/child interaction or any parent/child **power struggle**. The **outcome** will involve sending an **unspoken** message to your child that you **will** follow through after your direction is given or you **will not** follow through after your direction is given.

For example, let's say the directions you gave to your child were to put his dishes in the sink **before** he can watch TV. So you say,

"Johnny, put your dishes in the sink before you watch TV." Two minutes later he is watching TV and the dishes are still on the table.

So you say again (usually louder), "Johnny, put the dishes in the sink!"

He says, "Okay Mom, I'll do it in a minute…" and he continues to watch television…

Fifteen minutes later you see the dishes are **still** on the table, and you are so angry and frustrated that you **slam** the dishes in the sink and yell to Johnny,

"The next time I ask you to clean your dishes, you better do it!"

The **reality communication** of this parent/child interaction has **clearly** been established. The parent is frustrated, so she is unaware of the **unspoken** and **unintended message**:

> Johnny **does not actually "have to"** do his dishes **before** watching television. **In fact,** if Johnny gives his mom enough time, **she will eventually do it for him.**

*As collections of **reality communications** build in homes throughout **countless** daily occurrences, the **dynamics of *power shift*** from parent to the child*

In many respects learning how to get your child to follow your directions is like becoming familiar with a verbal or nonverbal form of martial arts. It is essential to have verbal/nonverbal "moves" that are **defensive, offensive, inactive, and proactive** (just as you would learn in **any** martial arts combat training). With this in mind, there are two ways to change these **unintended** messages sent to your child. They include the following:

1) **Stop allowing** his/her current strategies **to work!**
2) Have him or her **deliberately practice** alternative strategies.

Imagine that you are a movie director. The script has been written, and you have cast all the roles. You begin filming the movie, and the main character decides to say a completely different line than is written in the script. What would you do?

Say, "Cut," of course, and have them **redo** the scene!

Your life as the **leader** of your child is **no different!** From this moment on, I want you to have the mindset of you being the **director** of your life. Your children are characters in your "movie. As the movie is playing, if they **say** or **do** something that doesn't go along with "your script"...have them **redo it**.

What exactly do you mean by "it"? "It" means everything that is in the **human potential** and **age appropriate**! These are the only guidelines needed to make your child **redo** what he/she has said or done. The success or failures of these "redo's" are within **your** ability to control.

From this point forward, I will refer to these redo's as **scripting**. You can **script** for your child in two ways: verbally and behaviorally. This is how to apply them.

Verbal scripting

Verbal scripting is defined as replacing an inappropriate statement, question, or comment with an appropriate one. Whether it was his/her:

Voice Tone...

The child had an angry, whining, frustrated, or aggressive tone. His/her tone is sarcastic, mean, or unsympathetic to others.

Voice Volume...

The child's volume was too loud or too soft.

Rate of speech...

The child spoke too fast or too slow.

Give the child the words to help him or her successfully communicate any wants or needs...

Then...

Have the child repeat the words the **exact way** you directed *before* he or she gets the want, need, or desired activity.

As long as it is something he or she is **allowed to do/have**, it is **an appropriate time to do/have it, and** *the child said the exact script*, let him or her have the desired thing/activity.

Behavioral scripting

Behavioral scripting is defined as replacing an inappropriate action with an appropriate one. Whether it was the use of...

Silence/pauses...

The child is talking back when he or she should remain silent.

Hand gestures…

The child's hands/feet are too aggressive with another person. Or the child takes something without asking.

Body positioning…

The child's body is in constant motion or is moving sluggishly.

Body distance…

The child's physical body is too close or too far away

Show/tell the exact action that will help the child successfully achieve his or her wants/needs…

Then…

Have the child repeat his or her actions **the exact way** you directed *before* he or she gets the want, need, or desired activity.

As long as it is something he or she is **allowed to do/have**, it is **an appropriate time to do/have it, and the child performed the exact action from your script,** let him/her have the desired thing/activity.

<u>Warning system for verbal/behavioral scripting</u>

As long as there is no **physical fighting** or **danger** involved, give the child **three chances** to repeat the verbal and/or behavioral script. Only allow the child to have the particular desire or activity **after** he or she has **successfully redone** the verbal/behavioral script.

If the child is unable to achieve this within three chances, let him or her know that tomorrow is a **new day,** and try again then. If you want your child to take you seriously as the leader, you must make sure that you **follow through** with the limit you set for that day.

Remember, to **effectively lead** the scenario, you must be the one **least invested** in what your child wants in order to have **leverage**. If the child is becoming frustrated, giving an attitude, having a tantrum, or adding his/her own personal commentary, remember it is *the child's* self-regulation, not yours!

Chapter 12
Proper Feedback (You)

Feedback is defined as the messages parents **send back** to their child **after** the child has **spoken and/or acted**. The basic rules for providing effective feedback is to pay attention, make a comment, point out, and/or praise the words and actions you *want* him/her to **continue** to say/do. If you are providing them with feedback on the things you **don't want** the child to do, this is as useful as watering weeds.

In general, parents make **three** other common mistakes when giving proper feedback. They are listed below along with alternatives to give appropriate feedback to your child. They include the following:

1) *Mistake:* Parents provide meaningless feedback, such as: "That's great!" or "That's amazing!" or "Good job!"

    Alternative: Praise the **specific action and/or words** they used during that moment. This way he or she will be more likely to **repeat** the words/behaviors in the future. Examples: "I like the way you threw out the garbage right away!"

or "Excellent job sharing your DS with your brother!" or, "Thank you for telling me about your day at school."

2) *Mistake*: Parents praise or make comments on the child as a person, such as "Great boy" or "Good girl."
Alternative: Parents need to **separate the child** from his/her action. He or she is **always** a **good** boy or **good** girl. Give feedback on what he/she **specifically said** or something he/she did in **that** moment.

3) *Mistake*: Parents focus on **themselves** when they give feedback about their child. "You make **me** so happy/sad/angry/proud when you do that…"

Alternative: When a child is successful, ask how it feels. If he/she made an inappropriate comment or action, use verbal and/or behavioral scripting to **replace** his/her words or actions.

Chapter 13

Steps to End Defiance and Talking Back—Tonight

Children learn they are **allowed** to do something (or are given permission to do something) in two ways. The first way that children are allowed to do something, or they can have something, is that parents give their children **verbal** permission.

Example: Let's say it is dinner time, and you want your child to get a fork out of the kitchen drawer. One way to let the child know that he or she is allowed to get the fork is to say,

"Do me a favor, go into the drawer and get me a fork." That is the first way that the child knows that he or she has permission to take the fork out of the drawer.

The second way that children are granted permission to do something involves saying **no words** at all. Instead, permission is granted simply from **not stopping** the child.

Continuing the example above, the same child would be granted permission if the child goes over to drawer, takes out the fork, brings it over to the table, and starts using it to eat.

You see, if nobody tells the child to put the fork back, or nobody told the child to "ask Mommy before you take the fork," that child was given permission.

(This is the **subtle** and **sticky** way most children learn that they are **allowed** to do something.)

Many times, children **do** or **don't do** something due to the **second way** children are granted permission. Too often the things children **say** or **don't say** is because of the second reason as well!

You don't have to teach a child to say some of the things he or she says or do some of the things he or she does, but you can still give them permission to **continue** how the child is acting. How?

You give the child **permission** because you did not **stop** him or her. Nor did you give the child an **appropriate alternative** to whatever inappropriate words or actions the child used.

So, what you want to do instead is to **decide first** whether this is a *"yes"* or a *"no" moment*. What that means is, *Yes,* **I give** my child permission to say and/or behave this way. Or *No,* **I do not give** my child permission to say and/or behave this way.

If it is a *no* moment, there are **two steps** to make your child behave. If it is a *yes* moment, there are **seven steps** to make your child behave.

Over all children tend to behave the best when *yes* moments occur 80 percent and when *no* moments occur 20 percent of the time.

*How to handle a **no moment** (20 percent of the time)...*

I define "**no moment**" as something that your child is not allowed to do **at all**. For an example, with thunder and lightening going on outside, you would **not allow** your child to go swimming in a pool.

Another example: If it is snowing outside and your child insists that he or she will not wear socks, a parent **would not allow** that either. These are two examples that are pretty clear—the child is **not allowed** to have a want, thing, or desired activity.

A second way to define a *no* moment can also mean something that your child is **not allowed** to do for an **entire day**. For example, if your child hits his sibling over a video game, he or she should **not be allowed** to play with the game- for the **rest of the day**. Tomorrow, when your child can show that he or she can *keep his/her hands off* the sibling, your child can try again.

The **two steps** to handle a *no* moment are:

Step 1: Stick to the *no,* no matter how ***mean*** or how ***nice*** your child becomes.

It doesn't matter if your child says, "**I love** you, Mommy," or "I **hate** you, Mommy"; the answer is still *no.* So stick to the *no,* **no matter what!**

Step 2: **Redirect** the child to another activity. The activity itself **doesn't** matter.

(You can make suggestions on another activity to get your child's imagination going, or you can have your child figure it out on his or her own.)

Either way, when **you** decide it is a *no* moment, **you** make sure to redirect your child to an alternate activity.

Ultimately, **20 percent** of the time, you are going to have situations that are straight to the point, and the answer is *no*.

What you decide to declare as a no moment isn't good, bad, right, or wrong; **it just is.** Just make sure **both parents agree** on what constitutes a **no moment** and things will go more smoothly for the **whole** family.

*How to handle a **yes moment** (80 percent of the time)*

I define "**yes moment**" as something the child **is allowed to do**, but your child said or did something in **an inappropriate** way to get what he/she wanted. *Yes* moments have a strange quality to them that **appear as if** they should be a no moment.

This can be something as subtle as your child yelling at you to "Give me my juice **now**"; or the way your child talks back and stomps his/her feet at something you asked your child to do.

The fact is the **child is allowed** to have something to drink and to not agree with what you said. It is just **how** your child **expressed** his/herself that needs to be **changed or redirected**.

The **seven steps** to handle a yes moment are:

Step 1: Make sure you **model the words** and **behaviors** that **you expect** from your child. At the very minimum, stay **calm, cool, and collected** as much as possible.

Step 2: Make sure you **name the inappropriate words and/or actions** that the child **says** or **does**.

Steps to End Defiance and Talking Back—Tonight

Step 3: Make sure you **leverage** the desired want, thing, or activity. At the very minimum, leverage **personal space** and **body distance.**

Step 4: Make sure **you provide a verbal** and/or **behavioral script.**

Step 5: Make sure that the child does the **exact** verbal and/or behavioral script *first.*

Step 6: Make sure to **allow** the child to have the desired want, thing, or activity *last.*

Step 7: Make sure to **thank the child** for using the **exact** script.

Step One: Make sure you **model the words** and **behaviors** that **you expect** from your child

Modeling is so important. Making sure that you actually say the things that you expect your child to say and do the things that you expect your child to do, is the fastest, quickest, and most efficient way to get your child to behave properly. You see, children are like sponges. Not only that, they're also very **keen** observers.

For example, when somebody comes to your house and rings the doorbell and you go to answer it, your child, whether you realize it or not, looks to you to see how you interact with the person at the door. They're studying you; they're observing **you**.

Do you like the person who just came in the door? Are you unsure of the person who just came in the door? Is this your best friend? Is it someone you have known for years? How you behave makes a difference because your child watches and says, "Well Mommy thinks they're safe, so therefore **I'm** safe."

Unfortunately for you, parents, your child is doing this **all the time**. It's not just the matter of who's coming to the door as they look to you to find out how he or she should act and what he or she should say; your child is constantly observing you and constantly mimicking you. Your child will do things **exactly** as you do them.

Your child will develop *your* voice tone. Your child will develop **your** style of communication. He or she will mimic what **you** do, where you put **your** hands, the expression on **your** face, everything down to the tiniest detail. Your child is looking **to you** as the **leader**.

That's why, if you really want your child to say "please" and "thank you," it is really best that you say "please" and "thank you" as much as possible.

Similarly, if you want your child to eat fruits and vegetables as a part of his or her daily diet, it's best that **you** eat fruits and vegetables. Why is this?

This is because you can talk until you're blue in the face about the importance of saying "please" and "thank you," if you don't incorporate these things into **your own life,** you automatically communicate to your child he or she doesn't really have to do it.

Why is that? Because **you** don't do it. If it was so important and so critical, you wouldn't be talking about it, you'd be too busy **doing it.**

That is why when your child gets very frustrated and begins a tantrum and to lose his/her cool, the most important thing you can do is **stay calm.** It's very hard to do, however it's the most important thing to do, because right now your child is frustrated and has a problem on his/her hands that the child doesn't know to solve.

So when your child is flipping out and going crazy, if you start losing your cool, you are now in the same situation that your child is in. You are now frustrated with a problem that you don't know how to solve.

Now, your child is facing a totally different problem: He or she may not know how to ask for something that he/she wants, but you have just as much of a problem as he or she does because your child is out of control and you don't know how to calm him/her down.

So, if you want your child to be calm in his/her frustrating moment, you need to be calm in your frustrating moments, even though that moment is are about the child. The **faster you** calm down, the faster your child will follow **your lead.**

Step Two: Make sure you Name the inappropriate words or actions.

Most human beings, and especially children, lack a very important skill when interacting with others: They do not know how to **observe themselves** as they're **saying something** and as they're **doing something**. That's why talking and interacting with other people is important. We need other people to give us feedback on how to operate in this world.

I truly believe that the reason we aren't the best observers of ourselves is because we were never taught how to observe ourselves. In other words, adults and teachers went about giving us feedback in the wrong way. Specifically, there are two ways that adults gave us feedback incorrectly.

First, there was always a value judgment placed on what we said or what we did, and that value judgment always communicated a frustration, an annoyance, or intolerance for the way that we were handling a particular situation.

The second mistake that the adults made was that, as we were doing our best to problem solve and to develop in a very hard world, we were never told what to do **instead**. We were told: "Don't run," "Don't play with your food," "Don't jump on the couch," "Don't talk back," "Don't take things without asking," "Don't chew gum in school."

Please understand, this creates a natural conflict because it is **physically possible** to run, to play with your food, to jump on couches, to talk back to others, to take things without asking, and finally, to chew gum in school. We had no direction on what we should be doing instead.

I would like to take the time now to teach you how you can give the proper feedback to your children in a way that they won't feel rejected and in a way that shows them what they're doing, just as if you were holding up a mirror. It's actually very simple. The next time your child is running in the house, instead of saying, "Stop, don't do that! What are you doing? Why are you running?" you can say, "(Child's name), you're running in the house right now."

The reason you do this is because when children are at home and comfortable and excited, they might just start running, or they could be purposefully running. Either way, this shows them what they are doing and puts a mirror up to their actions without putting them down.

Ultimately, it's just like taking a Kodak picture that shows them what they look like because they can't observe themselves.

Step Three: Make sure you leverage the desire want, thing, or activity.

Continuing our earlier example of the child who's running in the house, what you want to do is to look at what the child is running to. If the child is running to his room after coming in to go play with his/her PlayStation, **that's your leverage.**

Use the fact that he wants to play with his PlayStation as leverage—not as a bribe, not as a reward, as leverage. So if you want your child to walk, there's something he needs to do differently to get to that PlayStation.

Remember earlier in the chapter when we talked about *yes* **moments,** and *no* **moments?** This is the time at which you observe the child's actions, or you listen to what the child says, and you first decide whether you will allow the child to do or say that.

If the answer is, for example, yes, the child can run to his PlayStation and nobody is going stop him, don't be surprised when the child is **constantly** running around the house.

Remember, children are given permission by not being stopped, and it is not the job of the child to determine the appropriate places where he or she is allowed to run. That is the job of the parent.

So if your child comes in the house and runs right past you, another thing you can use as leverage, if he is already up the steps and by the PlayStation, is **body distance** and **personal space.** If your child is far away, you go to the child.

You calmly walk up the steps, you ask him to come back down, and you have him do it again. If for some reason your child doesn't want to come, you can use personal space by taking his hand and walking him back down. This will create a reality communication that you will follow through on making the child walk in the house.

You don't need to do this too many times before the child realizes that when you say, "Walk in the house," you will follow through and make him walk in the house. That is the **power** of using leverage.

Step Four: Make sure you provide a verbal and/or behavioral script.

When we talked about leverage in the last section, I started to touch on number four with the example of the child running in the house. The behavioral script in that example is bringing the child back and making sure that he walks. You are replacing the inappropriate action of running with the appropriate action of walking; your child will **never** do it on his own.

Your child will not miraculously know what to do instead. Children are not mind readers. There is no number of punishments, there are not enough time outs, there are no behavioral plans or reward systems that will teach your child to be accountable. **You have to be the one to provide** that script.

You might ask, "How am I supposed to do that? Everything's just happening to me. You know, I'm going about my business, I'm preparing dinner, I'm getting the kids ready for everything, and this stuff just happens out of nowhere and it's completely out of my control." Sure, **in the beginning** it's going to feel that way because you're not used to looking for these moments to show your children how to replace an inappropriate behavior with an appropriate one.

Also, as a parent, you should never go into a situation without knowing what you want from that situation. So I suggest that you take out a piece of paper and write down the most common scenarios in which you find yourself unsure of what to do or how to handle yourself during stressful moments with your child. Take your time with it.

I want you to start with the **top three** and **prioritize** which one you find the hardest. Then sit down and pretend you're a movie director and write out the scenario. This time, as that scenario unfolds, I want you to write down some possible solutions and strategies on how you will make your child redo his behavior.

In the beginning, neither you, nor your child, will be perfect at this **and that is okay**. The first time you try this, you might not say it fast enough, or he might give you some resistance when you tell him to go back and do it again; that is perfectly okay.

Just like when you first learned how to walk, or ride a bike, or drive a car, in the beginning stages it is important to get in there, to do it again and again, and then to practice some more until you gain **mastery** over that skill.

Step Five: Make sure the child does the **exact script first**.

Before the child gets his/her desired needs met, or before he or she gets the desired wants or activities, your child **must** complete your behavioral or verbal script first. The reason behind this all has to do with reality communication.

If you provide a verbal and/or behavioral script and he or she doesn't do it first, then you're **wasting your time** as well as your words. You're actually speaking and putting forth energy for no reason. Let me give you another example.

Let's say it's dinnertime and you're getting your child's plate together: You're putting on the chicken, you're giving him/her some rice, some vegetables, and your child is saying "When is dinner? I'm hungry, I'm hungry, I can't wait, I want to eat, I'm hungry!"

You say to the child, "You will get your dinner plate **when** you're sitting in the chair." Let's say the child walks over toward the chair, but doesn't sit down. If you walk over and put the plate on the table and give it to the child when he or she is not sitting, you just spoke a minute ago **for no reason**.

On top of that, you created a reality communication in which the child can hurry you up and say, "Give me my food, give me my food!" You can tell him/her to go to the table and he/she doesn't have to do it.

So that's two unintended messages. Messages that I'm sure you're not trying to send your child, you're just so wrapped up in getting things ready that you don't realize you sent a non-verbal message that the child controls how and when he/she gets food.

If your child is in tyrant mode, he or she is going to want it now. And you just gave him/her permission and said, "Yes, you're allowed to have it the way you want it right now and **with an attitude.**"

If your child is allowed to treat their parents that way, the very people that **gave him/her life,** there is nothing stopping the child from treating **everyone else** he or she will meet the same way. So as the child's parent, it is very important to stress the order in which you do things.

If you tell your child to do something and there's a particular order, watch that he or she completes the appropriate behavior first before he or she gets the desired activity, thing, or want.

Step Six: Make sure to allow your child to have the desired want, thing, or activity **last**.

Step number six is really the **converse** of step number five. Remember, you've already decided, as the leader, that this is a yes moment, so there's no need to frame control.

You've already decided that, yes he or she can have it; your child just went about getting it in the wrong way. So in step number six, when you give your child the script and then he or she follows the script first, you need to **allow** him or her to have whatever it is that he/she wants.

Remember the story of dinnertime. Let's say you tell your daughter to sit down, and she is sitting there waiting for her plate of food and then you get distracted, or you go off and do something else and you never actually give her the food.

This communicates to the child that you will say something, but you won't actually do it, so the child sat down for no reason. It won't take too long for the child sitting down and waiting patiently for the food to see she's not getting it and to **stop doing the appropriate behavior**.

Your child will stop going to the chair and she will start to **bug** you. Your child will get closer to you because body distance and personal space is an extremely powerful way to have leverage over people who are bigger than us and stronger than us, but that's not the message you really want to send to your child.

The real message you want to send to your child is that she can trust that you will **follow through** and **provide** for her. That's what you want to teach your child

So it's so necessary to actually allow your child to get the desired thing, or want, or activity. This shows that you will actually do what you say and you say what you will actually do.

Step Seven: Make sure to **thank** your child for using the exact script.

The last step in this whole process is to make sure you show **gratitude** for what the child has done. When you say **thank you,** you are communicating to the child that your expectations have been met.

In other words, you're clearly saying the things that you like, the things that you want more of, and the things that you want to see your child do. Once a child has a **clear** understanding of what it is you're looking for, it will be **much easier** for your child to repeat those behaviors in the future.

Another reason why being thankful is so important is that **all children** want to please. Your child will never tell you that, of course, but **deep down** he has a need to belong, and because your child has a need to belong, he will **shift** his behavior.

Your child will change the things that he says and does to meet your expectations so that he will be welcome in the group. When you thank your child for something, your child knows **the direct way** to please you. When your child has this information, he will be much more likely to repeat that positive behavior in the future.

Plus, everybody likes to **feel good** about themselves; children want to feel like they did something right, or that they did something special. When you thank your child, he gets recognition for his action, and your child will feel good about what he did.

Now, you can thank the child for everything he does in the beginning, just so that your child can get used to hearing you say "thank you." In the beginning, your child may not be receptive and may not believe that you're actually thankful for what he did. In the beginning, **keep thanking anyway.**

As time goes on, you want to focus your "thank yous" on the things that your child has trouble doing or on things that are **difficult** for him. Let's say, for example, every morning your child runs down the steps when it's school time.

Every morning you get into a fight about running in the house, and your child still runs every morning. So you start doing these steps. First you stay calm and say, "Okay, Johnny, go back up the steps, I want to see you walk down," and he walks right up the steps, he doesn't give you a problem, and then he walks down the steps. So you should say, "Thank you for going back upstairs **right away**, and thank you for walking back down."

He'll make his way into the kitchen, eat his breakfast, and that will be that. So let's say the next morning he's coming down the steps and he walks the first attempt. That's the time you want to say to Johnny, "Thank you for walking down the steps the first time." This will communicate to Johnny that you're **paying attention** to what he does, and that the things he does actually matter.

When he feels important, and you add to that the fact that he really wants to please you, he will want to repeat that behavior more often. This, in turn, will make you want to appreciate that behavior more often, and you'll feel good about the relationship between you and your child. This is the power of gratitude.

Putting the Seven Steps Together

Ultimately, **80 percent** of the time, you are going to have situations *look* like the answer should be a *no;* however, with some **redirection** it can be a *yes* moment. What **you** decide to make your child re-say or redo during a *yes* moment isn't good, bad, right, or wrong; **it just is.**

Using these seven steps **repeatedly** will train your child to have a better attitude, say more appropriate words, and **cooperate** a whole lot faster.

Chapter 14
Effectively Leading a Conversation (Active Listening Skills)

About 90 percent of the time, it is **best** to effectively give your child clear, verbally stated **directions**. Let's face it, sometimes you have no expectations from your child except to **engage** in conversation.

Sometimes parents just want to know about their children and have them share their life experiences. How can a parent effectively **lead** the **conversation** during the moments his or her child is calm, cool, and collected?

The listening mindset

Your child needs two things from you to feel heard.

1) **Follow** his/her story from beginning to end, **without** interruption.

2) **Ask questions** about his/her story, thoughts, and feelings

(Free from advice giving, judgments, or solving the problem)

Often times parents feel that they have to give advice, fix, or solve the problem for the child to feel heard. You're an **effective listener** to your child simply by **providing a safe and comfortable environment** for conversation.

You can even maintain your own position and still **effectively listen** to your child. The following section will explain the steps to achieve this balance.

<u>Active listening steps</u>

To effectively **listen** to your child, you need to consider **five parts** of a story...

Intro...
(Prequel/any background information)

Beginning...

Middle...

End...

Update/Epilogue...
(Thoughts, feelings, and any personal commentaries)

As a rule of thumb, your child **must express** his/her story in chronological order **before** he or she can process the event. With this new insight, adults will be able to give their child the full time

Effectively Leading a Conversation (Active Listening Skills)

and attention he or she needs to share a story. The steps to actively listen include the following:

1. **Stop** what you are doing (Pick a time that is convenient for you).

2. Look at facial expressions and body language. Does the person look happy? Sad? Angry? Afraid?

3. **Restate** the events of his/her story (specifically thoughts or feelings about the story), or describe the facial expression/body language used as the story is told.

Repeat the **exact language** the child used.

Summarize his/her story.

Put his/her story **in your own words** (paraphrasing).

Remain silent. Look into his/her eyes/nod your head.

Ask **clarifying questions** that dig into the child's story.

(Who…What…When…Where…How…Which…)

Avoid asking, "Why"—it makes people get defensive

(**Tips**: Your child is trying to paint a picture to you with his/her words. He/she is trying to set up a "time machine" so you can go back into time **with** him/her and **experience** the event.)

Because most of the events are stories, moods, and settings you were not around for, he/she is attempting to have you "walk with the child" as he or she re-experiences an event.

What he/she needs **most** from you during this time is to **send back** verbal and nonverbal messages that lets him/her know you can...

- **Picture** what the child is describing from what the child saw;
- **Feel** what the child is experiencing emotionally;
- **Hear** what the child is emphasizing in his/her story;
- **Understand** the child's feelings, thoughts, and actions;
- **Relate to** what he/she has experienced.

When you can relate to his/her story because you experienced the same or a similar event, talk about it **after** his/her **full** story is complete. Too often adults jump into the story too soon to help their child feel heard.

Unfortunately, the child feels the opposite because he or she didn't get a chance to fully express the **five parts** of the story.

Instead of using **"me too"** as a strategy to prove you are listening, first hear the complete story, **restate** what he or she has said, then share your experience. Listening is a skill that involves sharing stories **one** person at a time.)

4. If you are **correct,** the child will say "yeah" or "exactly" or he/she will release **a sigh** or **calming breath...**

(Almost like a **reflex.** This communicates you are in tune with the person. If he/she **continues talking,** it is because you have **successfully** followed him/her thus far, and there is more to the story.

Effectively Leading a Conversation (Active Listening Skills)

5. If you are **incorrect,** the child will say "no," or "not exactly," **or** he/she sighs a **breath of frustration...**

> **Don't take it personally...**Hearing "no" means the message **you sent** back to the child is **different** from the message he or she was **trying to send you.** Be **patient** and **try again.**
>
> A mixed answer like **"yeah but..."** means that you have **some** of the pieces **right.** Be **prepared** for the child to **want to continue** as he or she clarifies the part you did not understand.

6. Repeat steps one–five until child feels heard. **Then** you can have a turn to share your stories or do something else.

Chapter 15
Conclusion
The Marathon

Whenever parents start a new program to change their child's behavior, something interesting happens. The child's behavior actually gets **worse**! You worked **so hard** to implement these new changes that experiencing **more frustration** makes you want to **throw in the towel.** How in the world does this happen?

This situation has a very **understandable** explanation. I would like to compare this **normal phenomenon** to a **marathon race.** A marathon race is approximately twenty-six miles. Let's say that before you learned the techniques in this manual your child's "behavioral endurance" was equivalent to ten miles on this course.

You were neither aware of these effective techniques nor of your child's endurance, so naturally you would think he or she would "fold" **instantly.** Just as **you begin** to **practice** and **your** "leadership endurance" starts to **build**, his or her tantrums "seem" to have intensified!

The reality is that he or she has **not** built stronger endurance; the child was never **pushed** to his/her **threshold** of **ten miles.**

Before now you only pushed the child **two–five miles**, but he or she **always** had more **endurance** than that!

At this point, seeing stronger defiance, tantrums, and attitudes makes parents want to give up...***Don't***! Keep pushing yourself and building up your leadership "tolerance."

With **deliberate practice**, you will soon get to nine, ten, even **eleven–fifteen miles**...and guess what? **Your child will fold!**

You just have to work until that shift in power becomes clear. That day will come, and if you **stick to it,** your relationship can change in a **few short weeks**!

That is **why** I have created the *Redirecting the Out-of-Control Child: Eliminate Defiance & Talking Back, Without Using Punishments, Time-Outs, Behavioral Plans, or Rewards.*

My sole mission is to **drastically shorten** the months (sometimes years) it takes to **restore order** in the home, **strengthen the bond** between parent and child, and **reconnect families.**

Thank you for taking the time **to let me share** this information with you and for **welcoming me** into your home!

About the Author

Jason Johnson, the In-Home Parent Coach®, has spent many years working with hundreds of challenging toddlers through teenagers diagnosed with ADHD, Oppositional Defiance Disorder, Conduct Disorder, Asperger's Syndrome, and Bipolar Disorder. He works with boys and girls (ages two to nineteen) with *severe* emotional/behavioral issues from various ethnic backgrounds, races, and religions.

Jason believes that parents are capable of gaining the leaderships skills necessary to restore order in the home, strengthen the bond between parent and child, and reconnect with their children. He is highly attuned to the leadership process and developing communication skills, and he has the expertise to point out effective ways to bring peace into the home.

His unique "on the front line of battle" experiences make Jason a powerful catalyst for change when working with families. Though reprogramming, exploration, guidance, and direct training, his clients learn to confront their fears, plan effectively, and take the necessary steps to reclaim their parental power.

www.ingramcontent.com/pod-product-compliance
Lightning Source LLC
Chambersburg PA
CBHW071712040426
42446CB00011B/2032